We All Want Love

Cameron Macdonald

FIRST COLOURCLOUD EDITION 2019

Part of the *Unified Love* Series

Copyright © 2019 by Cameron Macdonald

All rights reserved.

ISBN: 978-0-473-47140-8

www.WeAllWantLove.com

Twitter: UnifiedLove

To Denise and Amber

I love you both

Contents

Acknowledgments

For their support in bringing this little book to reality, I have many people to thank. I am sure you all know who you are without my mentioning every name, but particular thanks to Clare Wadsworth to whom I am truly grateful. If not for your lateral thinking and precision in editing, this book and its big sister *Voyage to the Heart: The Nature of Love* would not shed light on love at all.

Finally, I owe a massive debt of gratitude to my wife Denise for supporting my journey. I recognise your sacrifice and am truly grateful.

Preface

Of all things, why love, a friend asked after I published *Voyage to the Heart: The Nature of Love.* I had no answer. I needed to reflect. We moved on to another topic and drank more beer.

Before writing *Voyage to the Heart: The Nature of Love,* love had always felt imagined. When I was four Mum left home. Dad raised me and my two older sisters alone and worked hard to make ends meet. He rarely had time for us. Several childminders came and went over the early years, along with several women Dad had relationships with who also had children of their own. My sisters got on with growing up as did I, and we helped each other along the way — more them helping me than me them. We never said we loved one another except the love, Dad, Jeanette & Karen's scribbled in birthday cards, which seemed more custom than statements of love.

When I was old enough to seek out romantic love, I fumbled about optimistically and without much thought, like a hopeful goldminer without his lamp. At first dating was hard, but I learned as we all do. When I was 18, in 1986, I met my sweetheart, Denise, whom I love more than ever.

Looking back at my childhood, I realise that something was right when it came to love, even though we did not share a deep sense of it. Growing up was an anxious time, full of change, uncertainty, an absence of motherly love and too much self-sufficiency, but Dad was determined to hold the family together, come what may. He was always there when needed. He also had a stout sense of my and my sisters' importance, pricelessness so to speak, and defended the family against anyone daring to try to tear us apart. We were his family of whom he was proud. There was never any denying that. Keeping us together was the reason he worked so hard — why he spent so little time with us.

When I picked up C.S. Lewis' little book *The Four Loves* in 2006, I did not understand how Dad could have passed on any of these qualities of love to me, or even that they were qualities. Lewis' book promised to characterize and describe all the natural loves. This promise attracted me so strongly that I stood in a trance in the bookshop. Can love really be described? Will this book tell me if I was loved as a child? Will it tell me if I am loved now? Will it tell me my future on love?

So I was greatly disappointed when it failed to tell me any of these things, but what it did do was set me on course to find out what love is, why we love and how we love. Beyond that, it drove me to seek out the natural loves, and to characterize and describe them. In discovering these things, it became clear to me that my childhood was a loving one, despite my mother's absence.

On reflection, the answer to why I chose love of all things is because deep-down I have always needed to know whether I was loved as a child. This is not everyone's reason for wanting to know what love is, but it was my obsessive reason and, at a fundamental level, I now know the answer.

What you will find in *We All Want Love* is a story that answers three questions: what is love, why we love and how we love in a way that is easily accessible for those who, like me, want to understand their history of love, and maybe what the future holds in love. It does so by friends examining Part I of *Voyage of the Heart: The Nature of Love* over coffee. You need not have read *Voyage of the Heart: The Nature of Love* to enjoy this book, although you may want to read it now. For those who already have, this text will give you a second perspective.

To get the most out of *We All Want Love,* one should step back and look at the context of love for a moment. Love can be understood in two ways, just like an open sports car. The first is as an experience: driving along a country lane with the top down, your favourite music playing, your beloved next to you holding your hand, wind rushing through your hair, the roar of the engine as you change gear, the exhilaration of tight bends and the changes in the weather. You put the top up and the wipers on as a storm erupts overhead. Speed and exhilaration drop as you both weather the storm — one of many on your shared journey. You leave that road and move on to the rolling highway, enjoying the different pace and scenery. At some point you realize that there is more road behind than before you as you both fondly reflect on the love you share.

The second way to understand the car is mechanically. What is at its heart? What makes it start, accelerate, turn, slow, stop? Why does it overheat? What fuels it? Why does it break down and, when it does, how can it be fixed and by whom?

When looking at love as both an experience and

mechanically, its true meaning can be understood, and a true sense of whom we love and who loves us.

Clarity of mind means clarity of passion, too;
this is why a great and clear mind loves ardently
and sees distinctly what it loves.

—BLAISE PASCAL

NIKAU PALMS
WELLINGTON CENTRAL LIBRARY & CAFE

ARCHITECT: IAN ATHFIELD

I Am Love

Joanna's smile was so comforting. It has been such a signature of our friendship over the years.

"Enough gossip! Tell me about your work. Tell me about love," she said, pushing her empty cup and saucer to the centre of the table. The bitterness of coffee burst into my nose, filling my throat.

"Maybe another day. Let me get you another coffee and then tell me all about your trip to Oz." I stood up, reaching for her cup and saucer. "No, sit!" she huffed, "I'm happy with water."

She smiled, knowing my compliance was certain and finding it satisfying. "I want to know. You've been working on your book for so long now. So tell me, what is love?"

My mind stretched back to Fiji where this journey began, and how disappointed I was when C.S. Lewis' book *The Four Loves* didn't tell me what love is, and then how excited I was to think there was an answer after all. Love, regardless of type, has a common root, and all I had to do was get home and find it. But when I got home, all I discovered was a world fascinated with feelings and the romantic. Bookshelves sagged with self-help books and polished editorials as if only the thumping heart of romantic love were worthy of attention.

I turned to psychology as a body of knowledge, but found an obsession with feelings. Psychologists and psychiatrists were united in believing that love is reducible to feelings or emotions. Nothing I read told of a root set of feelings common to all love types, or a persistence of feelings describing love. More importantly, I could not find a theory where lovers chose to love or chose to hold back, which I knew intuitively was fundamental to love, so psychology failed to satisfy my search too.

It was in philosophy where I found thinkers who saw love beyond feelings and romance and, in a broader sense, as a choice. Plato, Sartre and Singer stood out and reduced love to its elements and the lover's aims, although none of them were easy reading and on their own they did not offer a complete theory of love that made sense. So I realized that I should develop and publish a coherent theory myself.

Joanna was sitting patiently.

"I'm not sure where to begin."

"Is love that difficult?"

"No. It's much simpler than you might think. It's been a long journey," I said wearily.

After sipping some water, she put her glass down placidly — placidly in that she exudes an essence of calmness that soothes. And yet this essence never undermines her purposefulness. She is always at peace with the world, but quick to call out injustice. It is these attributes that drew me to her when we were at school. She had an inner strength that I couldn't find within myself. Maybe that is why she took me under her wing, not that she would ever admit to that. She had left pink lipstick on the lip of the glass. "It's not a feeling," I said. She beamed her satisfied smile again as I sat waiting for a response, but her silence urged me on. "That's not to say we don't feel when we love," I reassured her, telling myself this was not a good start. I know telling people what love isn't puts me on the defensive. "When we love, we feel — well, most of us do, I'd like to think. Many feelings, in fact," I added, "but love is not reducible to one feeling or another, or even an emotion as modern films and songs would have us believe.

"A broken bone is not a feeling, although the experience of breaking one certainly brings about feelings.

Pain at first, and then intermittent aches and pains as the bone is set and mends. But, underneath, it is not a feeling.

"Have you ever broken anything?"

She shook her head.

"Except for a few hearts," I said.

"Who, me?"

"I remember Michael Peel. You were pretty mean to him."

"Who, Michael Peel from school? You remember him!? I think you might find it was him who dumped me. Heck, that was 30-odd years ago."

We smiled. "I've never broken a bone. But if it's anything like a sprained ankle, it's painful. Love is no different. Underneath the feelings people associate with love is something more fundamental." I hesitated. This is where people interrupt — or frown in disbelief. She remained quiet.

Reaching across the table, I grabbed a white paper napkin from the pile neatly stacked next to a little zinc-plated bucket holding salt, pepper and sugar sachets. "Do you have a pen?"

She searched through her handbag.

"It may be red."

I scribbled on the napkin to bring the pen to life. "It's

fine." I took a fresh napkin and drew the emotional layer of the three-pillar model.

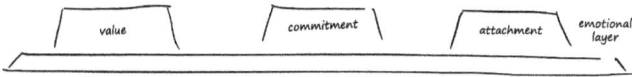

"When you say reducible," she said, "is that the theory you've been working on? I remember you saying you were looking for a universal theory of love, but I never really understood that."

"Good question. I have been looking for two truths if you like. The first is: when a person is in love — any person that is — a number of elements are always present. In knowing this, I know what love is universally as the elements apply to everyone in love. The absence of any element equates to no love. This is a universal theory — a general theory. The second is that for each love type all elements in the theory must be present with no exceptions. This is a unifying truth. A unified theory.

"When we reduce love in this way, it has three elements based on value, commitment and attachment — I'll explain in a moment — which complete the universal or general theory, and I have found 20 types of love in the West which unify that theory.

"The most important thing is that the three elements are necessary conditions. All three must be present at the same time for love to exist. If one is missing, love is gone or never was. The other crucial thing I found is that love when reduced is rational, although most of us think it is irrational — mainly because for centuries we have been telling one another it is a feeling or group of feelings which people think is beyond their control. But love is not reducible to the uncontrollable feelings most people describe as love."

I poured a glass of water, sipped, and looked into her face. She has soft crow's feet at the edges of her eyes that disappear into her temples. Her mascara drew my gaze back towards her brown eyes. I remembered a few weeks back — during late night drinks with a couple of our friends — her telling me what she thought about getting older. Postmenopausal women, she said — referring to herself — become unappealing: they lose their sheen, their glow, their vitality. Men become sweeter as their testosterone wanes: their hair thins and silvers, and their skin softens and becomes seasoned. I stayed silent, intrigued. Trying to understand how her perception had changed so much in such a short time. Up to that point she had always been so confident, and that I found comforting; she never doubted herself, her future, her beauty. The upbeat Joanna I had known since junior school seemed to be describing her future as a saucepan, which would not only lose its lid sometime soon but never find another. As I looked across the table, I thought of Rihanna singing about how we all want love. How important it is to be a lover's only beloved. And how we pursue the good in the warmth of a lover's arms. I had never thought Joanna would ever be on her own. Her life had always seemed so good from the outside. How could she not be loved?

"You do realise you will be swimming against the tide if you argue love is not a feeling?" she asked.

"The problem with love, or rather the problem with the word love, is we use it in two ways. It describes how we feel at times, and it's an expression of an enduring commitment to somebody we value immensely. I think this is why we are so tied to the idea that love is a feeling in the West. The phrase 'You love me now, but will you love me in the morning?' — or, as the song says, *Will you still love me tomorrow?* — epitomises the problem. I call it the adjective/verb problem.

"When you tell Stephen you love him, you are saying something more than how you feel at that time. And the same is true when he says he loves you. Those words are against a foundation of value, commitment and attachment. You view him as immensely valuable, as he does you. You offer him assurance to be there for him and do the kinds of things lovers do for one another, and he is your romantic beloved. This is love as a verb.

"In contrast, people say they love each other as an adjective when they mean, I feel this way when I am with you. That is not the same as saying I love you as a verb. The two meanings are distinctly different.

"The situation is made worse when we do bestow love and all that entails as a verb, because it usually includes the 'I feel this way' adjective. But, and this is important, one does not necessarily mean the other."

"I don't follow."

"Well, you can say you love somebody as an adjective but not as a verb. In the movie *Pretty woman*, for example, after sex, as Vivian lies next to Edward, she says she loves him. In saying this, she reflects how she feels there and then. Granted, she is close to the point of bestowing her love upon Edward in terms of wanting to be a part of his life as his lover, but unresolved issues prevent her from doing this, so she is not expressing her love as a verb, but instead telling him, or us actually, the way she feels as an adjective. Her saying I feel lovely right now, please don't make it stop, is a truer reflection of her state of mind.

"If we took all Vivian's feelings and stuffed them into a jar and stuck on a label, it would read 'love'. She is describing to Edward how she feels at that moment in one word, but she is not committing herself to him."

Reaching for her handbag, Joanna stood up. "I will have that coffee after all."

"Let me…"

"I'm good. Espresso?" She left the table before I could stand.

I thought in silence while she ordered, recapping. There were so many ideas swimming around in my head. Twelve years' worth. Love is simple, but it did not sound so.

I took the napkin with the beginnings of the three-pillar model drawn on it and hastily completed it.

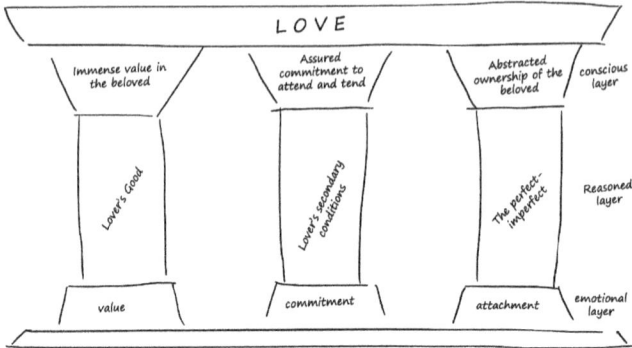

I noticed Joanna chatting to the waitress, her frame silhouetted against the backdrop of windows. Just for a moment I was reminded of Minnie, whom Dad had dated when I was a kid. He had dated a few women in the years after Mum left. Women of differing shapes and sizes, and characters too. Joanna was tall and slender, just like Minnie. I was five or six when she was around, so I remember little of her character, but I remember her wispy silhouette so well.

I thought back to the time Dad told me how he had struggled with Mum's leaving. He was not bitter, he said. He loved her. She rang him out of the blue from home when he was at work and told him to come home right away. When he arrived she was gone and me, Karen and my eldest sister Jeanette were alone. But he carried on. He worked hard and that took him from us, yet if we ever needed him — I mean really needed him – he was there; he made us feel life was worth the struggle — we were worth his struggle; he fought hard and held his family together because we were what he was most proud of.

He was giving me his vinyl records, including his treasured Linda Ronstadt album. She reminded him of his love of Mum, he said. He was so thin and gaunt. He was dying, but we didn't talk about that. Who talks about the painfully obvious? It was important to him that I had his records. He had played that album over and over through the years, and I never knew why until that day. The chorus of *Silver threads and golden needles* was running through my mind.

Joanna sat down. "Are you okay, Cameron? You look a million miles away."

"I'm fine." Taking a moment, I composed my thoughts.

"Are you sure? We can change the subject if you like."

"No, honestly, I'm good." Pointing to the model on the napkin: "Think of love like this. And before you say anything, art isn't my thing."

"It never has been," she giggled.

"Do you want to know what love is, or not?"

"I do."

"Three pillars of three layers. The first layer, Singer tells us, is this emotional layer made up of value, commitment and attachment. When we are falling in love — romantically, for example — we get to know the beloved in what Singer calls a process of *appraisal*. As we do, we become emotionally attached to them, and we develop commitment as we spend time with them. Think of this more as a concern — some call it robust concern and I prefer that as it describes the way we feel about them as we fall in love. And we come to value them as they become special to us. These three things — value, commitment and attachment — we don't think about to any great extent because we are too much in the moment:

falling in love emotionally — there are millions of songs, movies and TV shows, as well as non-fiction, self-help and psychology books on this stuff. I don't need to explain how it feels to fall in love and go all gooey-eyed. We've both been there. This is love, the argument goes. But we know it isn't. Love, as in 'loving', comes after falling in love — although if we think of love as an adjective describing the way we feel when falling in love as seen in *Pretty Woman*, this is it.

"At some point, at the end of falling in love, we recognise three things," I indicated the reasoned layer. "We find the beloved is good for us in that we think there is a good life ahead of us with them; they do the things we expect of them, and where they don't we accept those failures — this we consider meeting our secondary conditions; we recognise they are our one and only, or perfect-imperfect. When we appreciate these three things we decide to enter into a long-term relationship with them and say I love you. Behind those three little words is deep meaning." Pointing to the conscious layer: "You are immensely valuable to me; I assure you of my commitment to attend and tend to you, and I will hold on to you in ownership.

"This *posture* or state of being is rational love, as you

choose whom you love and whom you do not. Such bestowal stands above the adjective of love as it spans all love types and is universal to all lovers."

"Wow, that's a lot to take in."

I sipped my water and let her think on what I had said.

The Good in Love

Pointing to the bottom layer of the picture, Joanna said "But the emotional layer is all about feelings, so love is all about feelings."

"Love is an emotional endeavour, but we cannot be specific about feelings in a universal or unified sense. We're bombarded with messages that lovers, especially romantic lovers, bestow love because they feel the same as Vivian in *Pretty Woman*, but lovers can, in a rational sense," pointing at the top layer, "bestow love for whatever reasons they wish. That is if we consider love to be something other than a description of how we feel.

"When we were chatting so late the other week, you said love is hard work." She glared at me as if I should have forgotten that conversation. "What did you mean?"

"I meant there are times I can't be in the same room as Stephen. He makes my blood boil. I know with the changes I'm going through these days it's my mind that makes me feel that way, not my sentiment. It's not his fault, and it's not mine."

"But you love him?"

"Yes, I do. A great deal. And Angela too. I love them both."

"You're sure?"

"What do you mean, am I sure? You know damn well, I'm bloody sure!"

"When we have fallen in love, then bestowed love, and now love — whether romantically or platonically — we recognise we love. In your case, you believe you love because of your feelings for Stephen, and Angela too. And all the other people you love. But beyond those feelings, you know there is a sense of commitment and attachment as well. You also know you value them immensely. But in terms of feelings alone — do you know what underlying emotion any other lover might feel, have felt or should feel? Their feelings are as personal to them as yours are to you.

"In fact, we cannot be sure there are any feelings associated with love. Once a lover is past falling in love, they may not feel what we would associate with love, but they may still value their beloved immensely, continue their assured commitment to attend and tend, and zealously hold on to them just as they did on the day they first said I love you. Loving feelings, if there at all, are subjective regarding quality and quantity.

"All we can say is that the reasons behind love's bestowal, and ongoing bestowal are that the beloved should satisfy the lover in three vital areas. The first is the presence of the lover's good, which I believe for most lovers does include feelings, although they are purely subjective. I think this fair, because I am not so cynical as to believe love lacks emotion, even though it's fundamentally rational. The second is meeting the lover's secondary conditions, and the third the realisation that the beloved is the lover's perfect-imperfect."

Looking sternly at me, Joanna said "I don't find this appealing. Your version of love sounds selfish. I love my husband and daughter, and it's feelings that stir my love for them. I'm not looking to achieve some kind of good or hold them to conditions."

"I understand and I'll tread lightly. Let me explain what I mean by the lover's good. How much would you have given to be married to Prince Charming?"

She scowled.

"Sorry. Let's try this. If you could do it all over again, would you let yourself be swept off your feet by Prince Charming from the fairy tales? You know, the romantic ideal lover who brings health, wealth, glamour, no worries in the world from the moment you marry him?"

"There's no such person."

"Just run with me, Joanna, for a moment… okay?"

"And what, to have never known and fallen in love with Stephen and had Angela and loved this much and been loved in return?"

"That's the question."

"I'd choose Stephen, if it means holding on to him and Angela — of course."

"Why?"

"Because they mean the world to me," she said defensively.

"In what sense?"

"I don't understand."

"Does Stephen bring you wealth and health and take your worries away? Is he handsome and kind, the perfect man like the fairy tale prince I am alluding to? Setting aside Angela who theoretically would be at your side regardless. Prince Charming, after all, would have brought about Angela if she were what you desired."

"You know we're not rich, but we're not poor. He's a good man and a good father. And he makes me happy. Angela is half Stephen's, so she comes with Stephen."

"That may be so."

Her eyes hardened.

"You would forgo the greener grass of a prince's fortune in an alternate reality of happiness for your own harder life? It is this happiness, your current happiness, I refer to as the lover's good. The one that's all around you. Or rather, the good beloved and the good life that come together as 'your' good, which to you includes a wealth of feelings.

"On the other hand, it might be that a romantic lover could say I love you to their beloved and, in doing so, bestow love without any feelings specific to love. Their bestowal in that case could be based on quite pragmatic reasons, because their *good* is not bound to what you might consider feelings of love. In that case, the lover finds good in other things. Maybe political gain from a romantically intimate marriage like Francis and Claire's in the TV series *House of Cards*. Is it wrong to love in such a way that feelings are pushed aside and individual gains brought to the fore as seen in their loving relationship? Who are we to judge the quality of each lover's good?

"Listen to the song *Lyin' Eyes* for example, by the Eagles. The lover has bestowed her love upon an older man with wealth, but it seems there are no feelings of love. She has a relationship with a younger man for whom she feels what most people would call love. The question is, where does love lie?

"If asked whether she loves the older man with icy hands based on the good she enjoys in the absence of loving feelings, she would say yes, since she has bestowed her love and won't give him up.

"Regarding the younger lover: she has not bestowed her love upon him. The relationship is one of unrequited love, if he is waiting for her to tell him she loves him. Based on this, love does not lie here. Any feelings of love have not got past the emotional layer of the three-pillar model."

"So, you are saying she loves the old man with no romantic feelings, and does not love the young man with romantic feelings?"

"This is what the lyrics tell us. The good she finds is with the old man for other reasons, maybe emotional and maybe not, and this is the reason for her bestowal. She has not found the good with the young man and so will not bestow, even though she is driven by her feelings for him."

"I take your point on feelings. I've heard the song and seen *House of Cards*, but such love still sounds selfish and conditional. I don't expect anything from Stephen, and nor do I from Angela."

"We'll cover conditional in a moment, but when you say selfish you may be missing my point. What I am saying is you find immense value in a person who brings about a life, or a part of life, you consider good. It is not that you expect anything within this pillar *per se*, you simply recognise the good life, and as a consequence you bestow immense value upon the beloved, as you have with Stephen and Angela. And yet I am being a little careful here. Even though I am talking about the value pillar, this entire model is an ecosystem. The good you feel, and the immense value bestowed upon the beloved, comes about when the system is in balance and the capstone of love sits across the top. That includes recognising that your beloved must also be satisfied in their pursuit of the good too. Love is not something we do alone, especially romantic love. It is, as Singer recognises, a community of two. Nevertheless, the value pillar points to the fact that you weigh up everything. This is your good in sentimental terms regarding life with your beloved. When you recognise the presence of your good, you find your beloved of immense value, so love in this pillar is not as selfish as it may sound."

"But lovers do expect something, don't they?"

"And that is?"

"If they don't achieve the good life as you say, they will not appreciate immense value in the beloved and the pillar will not be built. Or, to put it another way, if they fail to get the good they once had, they will leave the beloved."

"I get your drift. When the lover recognises their achievement of the good, they recognise the immense value of the beloved, which creates the value pillar. And yet, as you say, if the lover no longer achieves the good, especially in outlook, they will not recognise immense value in the beloved and the pillar will fail. Yes, this means love is conditional."

"I thought so," she nodded self-assuredly.

Conditions in Love

"The good is not the only thing lovers seek to achieve," I said.

Pointing to the lover's secondary conditions on the napkin: "Before the value pillar fails, the commitment one will usually fail as the good life is intimately linked to the lover's needs, rights and values. That is: if your beloved cannot satisfy your needs, respect your rights or align with your values as a set of secondary conditions, your life with them will be negatively affected. But if they do satisfy you, and where they don't you can accept, you have a choice to make — because after all, on balance they give you the good life you seek and most of what you want. That choice is, do you stay or do you leave?"

"You make love sound like a contract."

"Do I? I don't mean to. Don't think love is a transactional affair, because it's not. When lovers get to 'if you do this, I'll do that,' and so on and so forth, then they are in trouble. But lovers do understand the conditions of their love from what they've had to compromise on to hold their relationship together. And, let's face it through bitter experience, you've dumped lovers you really liked because you couldn't accommodate failed conditions. We usually tell ourselves at the time that we're not compatible or there's no future there. In extreme cases, lovers recognise abuse is not acceptable and ditch their beloved when the right time comes. And as we know you've been dumped by lovers who couldn't accept conditions that you had no way of meeting, as have I. Maybe they really liked you in that adjective loving way, and you felt the same about some of the ones you dumped yourself."

"My love of Stephen may be conditional, as you say, but Angela's different. A mother's love is never conditional. It's natural."

"You love her because she's your daughter, right?"

"Yes. I mean no. You know what I mean. I couldn't imagine not loving her from the moment I knew of her."

"You mean you love her because of the relationship you have with her, not because of the genetic relationship alone? But you don't just love a random teenager in Auckland for instance?"

"She's my daughter."

"You love her as her role. She is your and Stephen's daughter whom you have years of experience with. Years that on aggregate have created your good, and create immense value in her. These factors are conditions that if taken away would contradict your love. But you also say you have no added conditions that would give you reason to withdraw your bestowal of love from her, and you argue no mother would conclude differently?"

"I do. And I get your point. Some mothers abuse their children. Abandon them. Kill them even, although they cry and break down and say they love them. But they do these things to them anyhow. I don't know why, and it breaks my heart to think about it, but you are right if love as a verb is out of choice. Do they have conditions that their children cannot satisfy? I don't know. But children are rejected by their parents. I get that although I can't see how any mother can avoid loving her child as an adjective and then not love them as a verb in your way, no matter how..."

A curtain of silence fell between us. She knew my past quite intimately, and I could sense an awkwardness between us where she felt she had intruded.

"I didn't mean to go down that particular road. I'm sorry," I said.

"Why are you sorry?" She looked confused.

"I'm sorry for making you feel uncomfortable."

"I feel like I've judged your mother. I didn't mean to be insensitive. I hate judging. I don't want to judge anyone," she said.

"You haven't judged me or my mother. With or without an understanding of the facts, I don't think we can say love should or should not be bestowed on anyone or anything, whether out of duty, virtue or some other outside pressure. The bestowal of love or lack of it is an act of free will that the lover answers for in their own way."

"I cannot imagine life without my mother being part of it. Or not being a part of Angela's. You were about four when she left weren't you?"

"Yes, just turned."

"You never really talk about it. Not to me anyhow. Does it feel like a part of you is... I don't know... missing?"

"I don't know what it's like to have a mother, if that's what you mean. She left so early in my life I cannot recall her. I knew I didn't have a mother when I looked at others like you when we were kids. I could see the difference. To me, growing up was full of uncertainty, anxiety, self-sufficiency, and without the maternal love I saw others enjoy, even though I had two older sisters who looked after me. Did I miss that? I envied it. I envied you. But could I miss what I never had in the first place? No. You can't miss the legs you were never born with. All you can do is wish you had legs like everyone else."

"It's so sad. Have you thought about finding her? To find out why. To understand why she left when she did. And why she stayed away."

"What good would that do?"

"But she must love you?"

"I used to wonder. Why do you think I'm so driven to find out what love is and why people love?" I looked Joanna in the eyes. "She has no reason to love me."

"You sound so… cold."

"I don't demand love. Nobody can demand love. And I don't seek it. How she might feel and her bestowal of love are not one and the same. Searching for guilt in her abandonment and seeking love's bestowal from guilt won't bridge any gap."

She sipped her water with a look of displeasure.

"Do you sense an absence of feelings from me when you say cold?"

Her eyes drilled into me from over the glass.

"Don't think as a rationalist I'm cold. You know I've felt the deep pain of love's loss and had the emotional marrow sucked from me when I've given my all in loving someone and been rejected regardless. And I've felt the wonderment of loving someone who has loved me back. I don't think love is cold or without deep emotional content. Understanding the nature of love as a rationalist does not ease the emotional agony of being dumped. Nor limit the wonderment of love when I tell my beloved I love them and mean it as a verb, and at the same time as an adjective in times of intimacy. What understanding love gives me is perspective. I know the difference between the verb love and the word used as a description of feelings. In my knowing these, I know if I was loved, when I am loved and if I can be loved."

Her comforting smile across the table made me feel for just a moment as though I were gazing into my mother's eyes. The mother I used to imagine as a child, who never left. I felt decades of anxiety and heartache well up inside me.

"It's okay, Cameron," she whispered.

"I'm fine." I was not, but I pressed on "Love is conditional," I said. "The lover's needs, rights and values must be satisfied. If they are, the lover offers assurance of their commitment to attend and tend to their beloved within the context of love." I pointed to assured commitment to attend and tend on the napkin.

"Assurance, commitment and the context of love? It all sounds… wishy-washy, formal and then contractual again."

"Joanna, love *is* wishy-washy. It's all about role and being with and doing things with the beloved in that role. You attend and tend to Stephen your husband in a different way to Angela your daughter, and you attend and tend to a friend differently again. And Chip, your dog, you attend and tend to him differently to the others. Angela attends and tends to you now and, as she grows older and marries, her attendance and tending to you will also change as your role matures in her mind.

"The only thing we can be sure of is that when the lover feels their secondary conditions are satisfied they offer assurance and do what is expected within the role they take up. This is what assured commitment to attend and tend means. To be there wherever and whenever the beloved needs you. And when you are there to support the beloved in their endeavours in pursuit of their good."

Joanna points to the lover's secondary conditions on the napkin: "And if the beloved does not satisfy the lover's secondary conditions?"

"Where love is not already in place, the lover must

decide how the future looks, how they perceive their potential beloved and the good life ahead, and if they can make compromises. If there is a considerable problem, they must decide if they can in good conscience bestow love knowing their relationship may one day fail. The underlying question will be how they feel about their achievement of the good they pursue and their perception of their beloved. In some cases, the lover will end the relationship, in others the lover will wait and see if things improve.

"If love is already bestowed, newly failed secondary conditions bring about reappraisal. I go back to your point that love is hard work. All lovers at one time or another are faced with the decision to either continue their bestowal of love or withdraw it. Has anyone in a long-term loving relationship, whether romantic or with a parent, child, sibling or friend, had a trouble-free relationship? One where there has not been the question of 'I'm just done!' When the needs, rights or values of the lover are not satisfied, reappraisal occurs. Sometimes a major breach of trust forces reappraisal, or incremental changes bring about the realisation that values no longer align or feelings have changed.

"If Stephen lied to you about something you thought

really important. This would cause immediate reappraisal on your part.

"Something similar happens with misaligned values where you might feel he no longer matched your values. You might ask yourself if his values had changed and if they could change back. Or if yours had or could change to accommodate his unchanging values? In both cases reappraisal may lead to more significant questions about the good life you pursue and whom you are pursuing that good life with. In both scenarios your conclusions depend on how you progress. Either you seek compromise with Stephen or find your secondary conditions cannot be accommodated and withdraw your assured commitment to attend and tend. This puts pressure on you to withdraw your love as the three pillars begin to fail.

"But just to reiterate the point, this doesn't mean at the emotional layer you no longer feel attached to him or value him and don't feel that sense of robust concern as before. These feelings will probably remain if they were there before. But the upper pillar has failed at the conscious and reasoned layer. This goes back to the adjective/verb problem we covered earlier. Lovers say 'But I still love him!' or 'I can't stop loving her!' The question is, do they love them regarding their bestowed love? Or are they saying: 'I feel this way about my beloved' in describing their love as an adjective?

"So, if the beloved meets the lover's secondary conditions — or where any are not met they accept such failures through compromise — the lover will recognise their needs met, rights respected, and values aligned. They then feel comfortable in offering assured commitment to attend and tend to their beloved. If not, the lover may withdraw their assured commitment to attend and tend and their loving relationship will fail."

Joanna's smile hinted she had crossed the gap from cold scepticism to warm understanding. "And when they do make such a commitment to attend and tend, don't they mean always or indefinitely or something like that?"

"In a romantic setting, the message across the West is forever. But that is an element of romanticism and cannot be applied universally to all love types. For example, comrade love is not indefinite. In *Voyage to the Heart*, you can read more on romanticism and the element of everlasting love, but these days shouldn't we be teaching our kids to avoid saying 'forever' in a fickle world? And 'never', come to think of it!"

Glancing at my watch, I see it is getting late. "Just on three. We should look at this final pillar attachment and how it relates to the perfect-imperfect."

The Perfect-Imperfect

I asked earlier if you would have taken up the perfect life with Prince Charming. You said Stephen is a good man and a good father. He makes you happy, and you would not have chosen the life of a princess if it meant losing out on the life you've led with him. I'd like to pick up on that if I may, and understand what being a good man means."

"I don't follow."

"Does it mean Stephen is good all the time?"

"Nobody is good all the time."

"And yet you say he is good, meaning the absence of bad in the same way I suggest the Prince is perfect, where he never does anything to bring about imperfection. Which means Stephen has been good at all times, to be good."

"That's wordplay. Stephen isn't good like that. He's not perfect. Nobody is. I love him to bits, but I'm not stupidly in love. When I say good, he is good, but no, he isn't good all the time. You know what I mean."

"And yet, you could have had the perfect Prince?"

"And then forgone the life I have had and still have with Stephen and everyone and everything that came and comes with that life. He is a package. Anybody you love is a package. When I say he is a good man and a good father, he is all that is part of being a good man and a good father. That is what's so special about him."

"Now you are older you know that living with somebody is far from a bed of roses, and Stephen is not perfect. He's in good company. Denise would be the first to tell you I'm far from perfect myself. Early in the relationship when you were falling in love, idealism played a huge role. If you can think that far back.."

"You make me sound old."

I smiled as the young waitress nudged in with a cup and saucer brimming with milky latte for Joanna and a clear Pyrex glass of pitch-black espresso for me.

"We're both old, Joanna. At that time you really were looking for your perfect beloved, as I was and Denise too, and at the same time you were building a view of Stephen as a person in his own right. Looking back... when dating, value is building. You are attending and tending to one another and, you know, doing the things lovers do without getting too personal, as well as becoming attached to one another and feeling a strong emotional connection between you. As you got to know him you discovered things you liked about him, and things you didn't. That's how it works when we get to know somebody intimately. As this happens, you apply two mechanisms to create what will become the perfect-imperfect Stephen. The first is the Stradivarius effect and the second the veil of assent.

"What's your favourite piece of music, Joanna? An instrumental piece?"

"As in?"

"Classical. Or a distinctive TV advert, or maybe a movie theme."

"Umm, don't laugh, but *Forrest Gump*. I really love the opening theme. It starts with a few piano keys and builds up to an orchestral melody. It makes the hairs on my neck stand up whenever I hear it. Silly really, but it's beautiful. I love that film — nothing like the book. It's hilarious."

"Remember the ape in space!" I said. We laughed. "The movie seems shallow, but it's a lot deeper than most people think. It's really about Forrest's infatuation."

"Infatuation? In what way?"

"He's like a lovesick schoolboy. He loves Jenny romantically, but he can't be in love with her. She won't let him. Not until the end."

"You think so?"

"There's an important sequence in the movie. She comes to his home and they spend what seem like a few weeks together. Then he asks her to marry him and she says he doesn't want to marry her."

"I remember that."

"And later that night she comes to his bed and they have sex…"

"And she says she loves him, but leaves him the next day while he is still asleep. I know," she says, "I've seen it so many times."

"Exactly! Throughout the movie Jenny refuses to allow him to be in love with her romantically. She will not reciprocate assured commitment to attend and tend and take up abstracted ownership of him as her romantic beloved. That's what she does the next morning. She denies him once more. But she does allow him to simply love her romantically like an infatuated schoolboy loves his teacher. That's until she finally reciprocates his love, when she realises she's dying and alone with his boy."

"I thought it was a film about friends. I never realised."

"You should watch it again with fresh eyes. It's about

the desire to move from loving romantically — infatuation — to being in love romantically. Luckily Forrest wasn't delusional where he was convinced Jenny did love him too. That would have made for a strange movie. Anyhow, let's get back to where we were — the Stradivarius effect.

"Imagine for a moment the theme of *Forrest Gump* played by robots and computers, which only play pure notes and chords in perfect time. That is, they don't play the piano, violins and the other real instruments used on the original soundtrack. They play electronic simulators that sound like those instruments, only they strip away all the imperfections of real instruments, leaving only the pure notes and their chords. They even strip away the little accidents and imperfections of the people playing them, instead playing off the music sheets at the exact times."

"I guess it would sound rightish. If that makes any sense?"

"It does, and that is my point. We expect there to be the right notes and chords, and within those we expect imperfections caused by handmade instruments. We also expect musicians to feel how the music should be played and introduce imperfections of their own so that without our realising it all these imperfections are woven into the music, making it sound right, as you say.

"In the same way, we know how the world works and that the ideal beloved will be imperfect. People don't always do what we want or believe in, all the things we would like them to, or value all the things we value. That perfect fairy tale Prince who does everything we want, when we want, how we want would be false. And when we want him to become imperfect in the way we want, even that would be wrong as we can't control it. It is intrinsic to the beloved alone, and frustratingly so. This is the perfect-imperfect that lovers uncover in those early days, weeks and months as they fall in love with their prospective beloveds."

"So, you're saying we think our beloved perfect while they are imperfect?"

"Nearly. The things the beloved does that make them who they are, make them, let's say, sound good and it is this good sound we maintain throughout the relationship. But here's the rub: that sound is specific to the lover's ears alone, as it is the lover who appraises the beloved and applies the Stradivarius effect — nobody else. So when you think I understand you when you say Stephen is good, I do when I also know that you love him. The lover applies the Stradivarius effect and creates the perfect-imperfect beloved, which in your language is the good Stephen. To somebody else Stephen is not that kind of good as they do not apply the Stradivarius effect as you do."

"If this is how we find goodness in our beloveds, why do we need two mechanisms?"

"The second accounts for the fact that people can fall out of tune if we continue to use the musical analogy."

"In what way?"

"Over the years you have come to know Stephen intimately and have a collection of memories that define him." She continued to look confused.

"If I were to ask which attributes define Stephen, what would you say?"

"I'm not sure."

"Kind would be one attribute I think you would give as a virtue. You might say handsome in an aesthetic sense. You also said earlier he is a good father."

"Oh, I see."

"By considering all you know about him, on aggregate he is good. Good enough to sound sweet when you apply the Stradivarius effect. As we have ascertained."

She smiled. "That sounds right. But not perfect. Just

perfect-imperfect."

"Yet if he does or says something that significantly changes the way you perceive him to be, your view of him will change. No longer will he sound sweet or good, and no longer will he be your perfect-imperfect."

"I'm trying to get my head around what you mean."

"Let's say, perish the thought, he has an affair. Even though none of his other attributes have changed, the aggregate has, because cheating is significant. Even with the Stradivarius effect applied, your new tune would not be good."

"So the Stradivarius effect smooths out minor imperfections, but it cannot smooth out significant ones?"

"Exactly. Many lovers overcome significant negative shortcomings in the beloved by using the veil of assent to create and maintain the perfect-imperfect, where otherwise the beloved would be marred by a polluted identity.

"A veil? You're losing me again."

"Imagine you have a translucent veil in front of your face that acts as a filter. It allows in attributes of Stephen you wish to acknowledge and keeps out those you wish to avoid.

"By bringing through the attributes you wish to apply the Stradivarius effect to, you ensure Stephen sounds good and maintains his perfect-imperfection.

"This is absolutely necessary for love as the lover puts immense value in the perfect beloved who unlocks the perfect life — or the perfect-imperfect beloved whom the lover lives the good life with."

"This sounds delusional. If Stephen had an affair, pretending he had not by leaving the fact outside a veil would not take away the fact he had, so he would not sound good to me."

"I may have used a bad example in your case. An affair for some lovers might be so significant it could not be left outside the veil. It must come inside. When it does, the beloved's identity becomes polluted and they in turn become irreparably imperfect. Then the attachment pillar fails, and with it the model fails and the lover withdraws their love.

"Yet even though some attributes are significant, they can be remedied with the veil. This refers to any type of lover, not specifically a romantic lover. Friends, for example, can put each other in a situation where the veil of assent and Stradivarius effect have to be used to remedy a relationship that would otherwise founder. One friend may breach another's trust for example. The veil may be used to leave this outside in context of why it happened and the understanding it will not happen again. Once the breach of trust as an attribute of the beloved's identity is left outside the veil, the Stradivarius effect smooths out the beloved to perfect-imperfection once more.

"Back to your point: this is delusional. You may interpret it as such, but I would say that just because attributes can be left outside the veil does not mean they are forever forgotten. The underlying point is that attributes left outside are not considered relevant to the lover's bestowal of love. They are therefore suppressed from the beloved's identity, but not erased. We know this to be true where love breaks down and these attributes are used to character assassinate an ex-beloved by an ex-lover. This does not always happen, but part of falling out of love can include turning the perfect-imperfect to the imperfect. Lovers do this by bringing suppressed attributes into their veil, dropping the Stradivarius effect and thus poisoning the identity of their ex-beloved. It's not pretty, but it happens.

"If we put this pillar together at the emotional layer, we become attached to the beloved as we get to know them intimately when dating. At some point, we recognise how good they are through both the Stradivarius effect and veil of assent and they take on perfect-imperfection, which supports the good life we seek. Once we realise this, we take ownership as we bestow love upon them.

"This last point brings us to the final aspect of the model. Possession of the beloved." I paused for thought and drank some of my bitter espresso.

"Singer said in one of his MIT lectures that love is about boys chasing girls until one of the girls catches one of the boys. That comment has stuck with me for a long time as there is something not quite right."

"And?"

"What is the good of capture without captivity? Plato is clear that we seek to possess the good, but if we have captured the good as Singer says, we must hold on to it — or them, right? Lovers do this by taking abstracted possession of their beloveds once they recognise that they have found their perfect-imperfect. And, on their side, beloveds embrace this ownership."

"No. You're wrong. As a woman, women have been rejecting ownership by men for years, and now you are telling me I seek it."

"In a sense, yes. But ownership is abstracted, even though it is often confused with the oppressive kind of ownership you are alluding to. To give you an idea of what I mean, in Rhianna's song *We All Want Love* — a beautiful song by the way if you've never heard it — she says as a beloved she seeks to be owned."

"I know. I've heard it. And it's deeply saddening that Rhianna seeks ownership when she has suffered terrible domestic violence linked to jealous ownership."[1]

"I understand, and maybe Rhianna does too. The ownership she seeks as a beloved is not one of oppression in terms of barefoot and pregnant. It's not one of servitude. Nor does she want to be trapped like a rare exotic bird in a cage. Her ownership is one of abstraction in the mind of the lover in recognition of her status as the perfect-imperfect. It is a passionate acknowledgement that she is somebody's beloved and that they can be relied upon to attend and tend to her because they value her immensely. Here the lover acknowledges the beloved to be their girlfriend, wife, husband, daughter, cat, friend, God, country, car — you name it. In the lover's mind, possession means to hold on to the immensely valuable goodness the beloved is to the lover.

"But abstracted ownership should never mean possessiveness in regard to denying the beloved of their own good either. This takes me back to a point you made earlier about the lover's selfishness in seeking their own good. If the beloved does not achieve their good, they will reject the lover who in turn will not achieve theirs,

---

[1] Referring to Rhianna's alleged assault by Chris Brown, 2009 (CNN: http://edition.cnn.com/2009/SHOWBIZ/Music/06/22/chris.brown.hearing/)

and the whole three-pillar model will fail. There should be recognition that what hurts the beloved hurts the lover. Ownership within the model includes robust concern at the emotional layer. Not only is the whole three-pillar model one ecosystem, but where love is requited there are two models running in parallel that rely on one another as a greater emotional ecosystem.

"And so, stepping back, this final pillar's completion in taking up abstracted ownership of the perfect-imperfect beloved brings together an ecosystem of love. All that remains are the words I love you, or equivalence for non-romantic and religious loves, and with these words the capstone of love is placed across the top. This creates the loving relationship."

"That's a lot to take in late on a Tuesday afternoon," she said.

"In some respects, it is, but all I've said at a most basic level is that when someone loves you, you are valued immensely because that person is committed to your welfare and wants nothing more than to have you in their life. In line with these points, don't confuse the adjective of feelings associated with love with the verb love. Nor falling in love with being in love. Finally, loving someone is a choice. A choice based on the good you achieve, your secondary conditions met, and the beloved being the perfect-imperfect you find through appraisal.

"Regarding feelings, we may bestow love because we feel what is described as loving feelings, or we may bestow love in the absence of such. It's up to the lover. This is not to say love is not an emotional experience. I think all intimate relationships, especially loving ones, are emotionally bound, but this does not mean love is reducible to one feeling or another. Nevertheless, love is bound to the possession of the good life with the good beloved, and that in itself is purely subjective in terms of feelings attached. But — and here is the takeaway — at its core your love is a bestowal of immense value, assured commitment to attend and tend and an uptake of abstracted ownership of your beloved. This is the verb to love, and this you do out of choice.

"I hope I answered your question on what love is?"

She looked satisfied and at peace as she tucked the paper napkin with the three-pillar model scribbled on it into her handbag. "I'll read your book."

We put on our coats and left the café. Frigid air bit at my cheeks in the busy street as we embraced briefly. "We'll catch up next week," I said, breathing in the subtlety of her expensive perfume.

"We will."

I joined the throng heading for the railway station and pulled my coat collar further up, wondering if I were right about never looking for Mum. Then I stopped and thought for a moment. Life is good? "Yes!" I said to myself. "I'm loved enough."

www.ingramcontent.com/pod-product-compliance
Lightning Source LLC
Chambersburg PA
CBHW071423040426
42445CB00012BA/1281